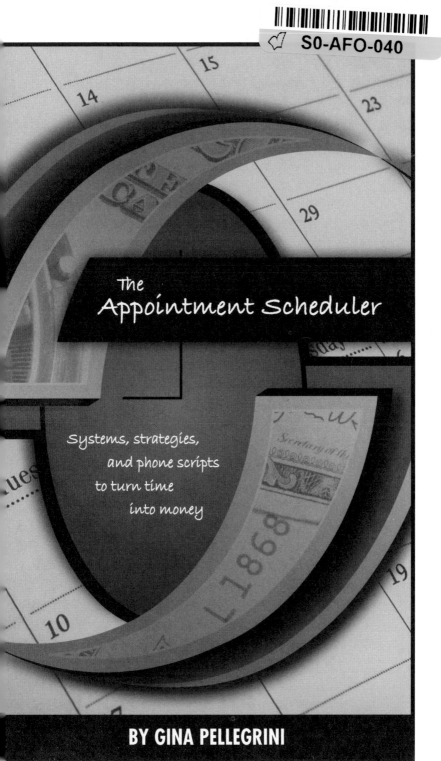

The
Appointment Scheduler

Systems, strategies,
and phone scripts
to turn time
into money

BY GINA PELLEGRINI

This book is dedicated to my brother and friend, Perry Pellegrini. Perry lost his battle with cancer in February, 2005. For me, he was a source of support, humor, and unwavering loyalty. Perry was loved by many and is greatly missed.

TABLE OF CONTENTS

ACKNOWLEDGMENTS

Ten years ago, I dreamed of writing a book, but thought it was impossible. Now, here I am today with my third publication, and I can't wait to get started on the next one.

None of this would be possible without my friend and writing partner, Lynne Crist. Lynne has the magic touch when it comes to clarifying my ideas and editing the text. Bottom line, I could not do it without her, and I am extremely grateful for our collaboration.

I also want to acknowledge my Coach 2 group, with Dan Sullivan and Babs Smith, for challenging me to aim high in everything I do. A big thanks goes to my friend Shannon Doyle who always asks the right questions as I chart a course for my company. And finally, I want to recognize Lisa Sauer, my right arm, who manages the office with care and efficiency and supports me as a true friend.

To get the most out of *The Appointment Scheduler*, producers should read the book carefully, taking notes, highlighting key points, and thinking about how to apply the new systems. Marketing assistants should take notes as well, giving special attention to the scripts in Chapter Nine. When finished with the book, the producer and marketing assistant should schedule a time to discuss the main points and develop a game plan. A game plan consists of proposed changes, the rationale behind them, the anticipated results, and a time frame for action.

After that comes the real work -- implementing the game plan. If you use what you have learned in *The Appointment Scheduler* and stick to your game plan, you will write more business with top prospects and clients.

When Gina Pellegrini told me she was writing a book on appointment scheduling, I was more than happy to provide the Foreword. As a General Agent in Chicago, I created the One Card System, a method of scheduling appointments by working the producer's client base. Under this system, all appointments are made by a trained marketing assistant. The approach makes sense because a producer's job is to get in front of people and *sell*, not call for appointments. Also, marketing assistants often get better results because they are in the office when people call back. They have more time to talk and develop a long-term relationship.

Years ago, when Gina worked as an assistant in my agency, I was impressed with her straight-talking style and initiative. I asked her to start a training program for marketing assistants in the agency. The program was a success, and I am not surprised that today Gina runs her own thriving consulting business. She has a gift for working efficiently and motivating business owners and their staff.

Like Gina, I have always encouraged people to realize their full potential. I believe marketing assistants are capable of taking on more responsibility in the sales cycle. With the right training, they can make all the calls, set up all the appointments, and effectively manage the producer's calendar. My One Card System encouraged marketing assistants to pursue *all* leads, not just certain prospects or favored clients. That way, the producers could focus on uninterrupted selling.

In *The Appointment Scheduler*, Gina explains how to work the client base to schedule appointments with the right people. Her practical approach can help marketing assistants and producers achieve a higher level of success. I believe everyone in the financial services industry can benefit from Gina's book.

Al Granum
Granum Agency, Inc.
Downers Grove, IL

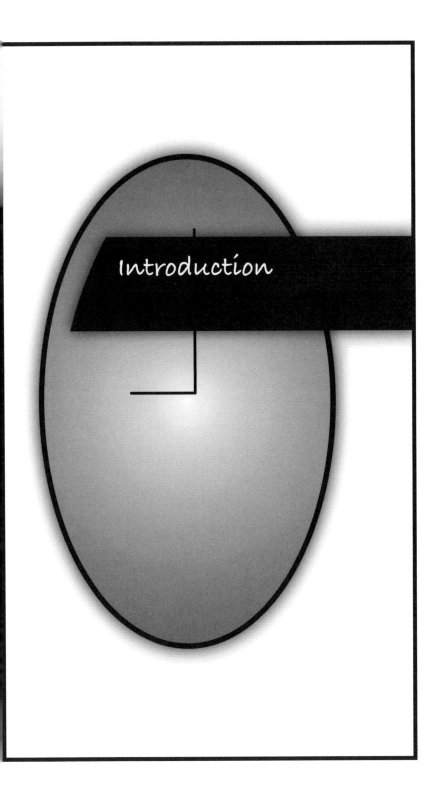

Introduction

The groundwork for *The Appointment Scheduler* was begun at The Granum Agency in Chicago where I was hired as a receptionist in 1975. Untrained but ambitious, I knew from the start that I wanted a more challenging position. One day when I heard about an opening for an assistant (or secretary, as we were called back then), I went for it.

I met with Tom Walder, a producer with Northwestern Mutual who was just starting out in the business. The "interview" was brief. Tom hired me in five minutes, after asking if I could type, file, and answer the phone.

On my first day of work, Tom didn't say much. He simply asked me to call some clients to schedule appointments. In a mild panic, I thought, "How do I do that? Why am I calling? Who are these people? What if they all say no?" (Actually, just as puzzling -- "What if they say *yes*?")

Taking the plunge. Luckily, I was naïve enough to pick up the phone and give it a try. I said, "Hi. This is Gina from Tom Walder's office. I am calling to schedule an appointment for you to meet with Tom. How does your schedule look?"

Of course, the people on the other end of the line asked why Tom wanted to see them. I was honest and said I had no idea because it was my first day on the job. Despite (or because of) my obvious inexperience, I made six appointments in one hour.

When Tom returned to the office, I told him my results. He said, "Great! You're hired." Confused, I said I thought I already had the job.

Tom replied, "Al Granum believes a good assistant can do a lot more than type and answer the phones. I wanted to see if you could do more." Tom went on, "Al says producers need assistants who will keep them in front of the right people. That's a big part of your job. Pushing paper won't make us any money, but keeping me in front of prospects and clients will."

After some time on the job, I became a master on the phone and scheduled *all* of Tom's appointments.

My own consulting business. I have come a long way since then. I left Tom's office after seventeen successful years and started my own consulting business, #O.N.E. CONCEPTS. Based in Minneapolis, our company specializes in small business management and employee development.

One of our services is to teach marketing assistants how and when to call for appointments on a regular basis. As part of the training, we developed (and continue to refine) specific telephone techniques aimed at existing clients, referrals, prospects, seminar attendees, and cold calls. Over the years, we have seen how consistent appointment scheduling leads to an improved bottom line.

Years of experience. This book is the result of twenty-five years of experience in the financial services industry. It contains the systems and scheduling techniques I once used on the job and now teach to marketing assistants across the country.

I should point out that I made a conscious decision to use the term "producer" throughout the book. Although other titles are appropriate for people in the financial services industry -- e.g., agent, advisor, or planner -- I opted for "producer." My insurance background no doubt influenced my choice.

Try it. My approach to appointment scheduling is not the only one out there, but it definitely works! Try it, and I believe you will experience a significant increase in appointments and production.

Gina Pellegrini
#O.N.E. CONCEPTS

Chapter 1

Why Hire a
Marketing Assistant?

If you want to grow the business, what is the best way to spend your time -- scheduling appointments or actually meeting with people?

Have you ever walked into the office on Monday morning and stared at an empty calendar? The week before, while you were busy selling, you didn't have the time or energy to make calls. Now your calendar is wide open, and you have to play catch-up by getting on the phone to schedule appointments.

Time management is one important reason for hiring a marketing assistant. Think about it. If you want to grow the business, what is the best way to spend your time – scheduling appointments or actually meeting with people?

Spending time and money. Effective time management is the cornerstone of a successful business. You know the saying "Time is money." But do you know how it applies to your business? Are you spending time on the right things? Another adage is "To make money, you have to spend money." Again, how does that apply to you? Are you spending money in the areas that will ultimately boost your profits?

From what I have seen, many people are confused about time and money. As a consultant, I work with business teams across the country to improve systems, communication, and workflow. Over the years, I have visited dozens of offices and have dealt with all kinds of business issues. One issue is surprisingly common. I have found that producers will readily spend money on *things* -- computers, printers, phone systems, etc. -- but not on personnel capabilities that could save time.

By capabilities, I mean specific skill sets in employees. Doesn't it make more sense to spend money on the people who shape your success? In my opinion, when you invest in your employees, you are growing the business. Training and development lead to better organization, defined roles, and greater efficiency. For a producer, the benefits are clear. By developing your staff, you are freeing up your own time for *selling*, which is what keeps your business going.

Spending money on staff. Marketing assistants can bring consistency to the sales cycle. Without them, producers face uneven scheduling and unwanted down time. Sustained, future success depends upon delegating the scheduling role to someone else. In other words, to make money, you need to spend money -- *on a marketing assistant*.

When Tom Walder hired me as an assistant, I had to prove I was worth the expenditure. Like many producers, Tom was concerned about the *cost* of employing an assistant. He knew he needed staff, but did not like the idea of meeting a payroll and spending time on training. However, once I took over the appointment scheduling, it did not take long to prove myself. I made calls every single day, working Tom's client base and booking appointments on a regular basis. Tom soon saw the connection between my daily calls and improved sales results.

Regular scheduling. Regular -- meaning *daily* -- appointment scheduling is the key. Chances are, you have a marketing assistant who could develop the specific skills and mind-set to schedule all your appointments over the phone. Or you may need to hire someone new to get the job done. In either case, someone else can make these calls, and the appointments will lead to increased revenues for the business.

THE ADVANTAGES OF HIRING
A MARKETING ASSISTANT

- If marketing assistants leave a message, they are more likely to be in the office when the referral, prospect, or client calls back.
- Marketing assistants often develop a rapport with prospects and clients.
- Marketing assistants can build an alliance with a client's support staff.
- By managing the calendar -- and providing consistent sales opportunities -- marketing assistants become a significant part of the company's growth.
- During phone calls, marketing assistants are selling just one thing: the appointment.

The time-money connection. My purpose in writing *The Appointment Scheduler* is to provide you with the systems, strategies, and phone scripts to turn time into money.

How do you find the right marketing assistant? Look for some answers in Chapter Two.

Chapter 2

The Search for the Right Marketing Assistant

The ideal candidate is someone who is assertive and willing to overcome objections on the phone.

Before going any further, let me clarify the term "marketing assistant." Many people see the word "marketing" and think of ads, brochures, and newsletters. In this book, however, "marketing" refers specifically to appointment scheduling. Marketing goals are a full calendar, a stronger relationship with clients, and an increase in revenue.

Finding the right marketing assistant for your business is relatively easy if you are clear about your needs and objectives. What exactly do you want your marketing assistant to accomplish? When? How? Give the position some careful thought before posting a want ad and gathering resumes. Your search will be much smoother if your expectations are unambiguous.

First, think about the parameters of the job. Ask yourself:

- Who will the marketing assistant call, now and in the future?
- Can I let go and have the marketing assistant make all of my calls?
- How long will the marketing assistant be on the phone each day?
- How will the marketing assistant be held accountable for results?
- How and when should the marketing assistant be terminated if results are not produced?
- How will the marketing assistant be paid -- salary, or salary plus incentive based on results?
- Who will train the marketing assistant?

The Search for the Right Marketing Assistant

- How will the marketing assistant gain credibility with clients?
- How will I find the candidates?

Once you have answered these questions fully and honestly, you can create an ad.

(If you feel overwhelmed, help is available. Interviewing and hiring are covered in depth in another product of mine, *The Personnel Package.* Refer to our website at www.oneconcepts.com for more information about our hiring products and services.)

> *"The best executive is the one who has sense enough to pick good [people] to do what he wants done, and self-restraint to keep from meddling with them while they do it."*
> *Theodore Roosevelt*

The ideal candidate. The ideal candidate is someone who is assertive and willing to overcome objections on the phone. The ultimate team player, this person must be good at building relationships. It also helps to have some retail, sales, or telemarketing experience. A marketing assistant must understand the purpose of the job, which is to schedule appointments, *not* sell products.

Posting an ad. In your ad, explain what the marketing assistant will do and what experience is required. Include a general description of your business. As a rule, it is better to steer clear of the term "marketing assistant." Again, "marketing" means different things to different people. To avoid confusion and to get a response to the ad, refer to the position as "administrative sales assistant." Here is a *sample* want ad that gives you an idea of the basics:

ADMINISTRATIVE SALES ASSISTANT
Established financial services office in (city and state) seeks a self-starter with industry knowledge to manage producer's calendar and client base. Duties include scheduling appointments with new and existing clients; handling incoming calls and correspondence; overseeing appointment preparations; maintaining top client relationships; and performing various administrative duties. Must be computer literate, detail-oriented, and capable of multi-tasking. A positive attitude and good communication skills are a must. Email your resume to (email address). Include salary requirements and a paragraph on why you are qualified for this position.

Prescreening. One week after placing the ad, gather the resumes you have received. Review all of them at the same time, not as they come in. After carefully reading the resumes, prescreen the top candidates over the phone. Prescreening saves time by weeding out candidates with incompatible skills or income requirements.

Some key questions to ask during the telephone prescreening process:

- Why does this position interest you?
- What are the duties in your current position?

- Why do you want to make a change?
- What is your income range? What is your current salary?
- Have you ever done phone work to sell products or ask for business?
- Why would someone want to hire you?

When you find three to five people who have the experience and take-charge attitude you want, schedule the face-to-face interviews.

The interviews.   The first round of face-to-face interviews will give you a general idea of the candidates' abilities, personalities, and reasons for applying. Evaluate their people skills and confidence. Are they personable? Do they seem motivated? Do they have a firm handshake? Remember, what you see during the interview, a client will *hear* on the phone.

Testing/role-playing. If after the first interview, you think a candidate has promise, give him or her the script for calling referrals. Tell the candidate to go home, read over the script, and practice the language. Then if the candidate is serious about the job, he or she should call your office to set up a time to role-play over the phone. The candidate might want to schedule an in-person session, but I recommend a phone call. It is easier than a face-to-face situation, and more important, it measures the necessary skills. After all, the point is to see how well the candidate sounds on the telephone.

I should warn you, some people will not call back after reviewing the language. If they don't, it is probably a sign that they aren't right for the job. If candidates are afraid to try role-playing, they might hesitate when it's time to phone clients or prospects.

To begin the role-playing, I suggest you play the part of the marketing assistant. You will "call" the candidate who will refer to the scripts for objections to scheduling an appointment. By playing the client, the candidate will get a better feel for the calls. You will respond to each objection with language from the scripts, and the candidate will learn how to overcome resistance. After you role-play with the candidate one or two times, reverse roles.

Sample scripts. Sample scripts for role-playing are found in Chapter Nine. Remember, you are not looking for perfection in this first attempt by the candidate. Instead, you are looking for perseverance and the ability to think on one's feet. You are also looking for a professional style that best represents your business. Marketing assistants should project friendliness and competence over the phone. You want someone who is respectfully persistent with clients and prospects. You are looking for a character trait -- tenacity -- and also a personality trait -- sociability.

It is *not* easy. People who have never called for appointments think it is easy -- almost like answering the phone and directing a call. But it is *not* easy. If calling were easy, producers would have full calendars all of the time, and you would not be reading this book.

During the role-playing, you will determine if the candidate can really do the job. Making appointments with existing clients is the least complicated assignment, while cold calls and referrals are harder. You can learn a great deal about the candidates by the way they handle typical questions and obstacles.

Be clear about the job duties. Discuss the expected number of phone calls per day, the types of people called, and the required results. If the candidate is comfortable with your expectations, discuss the specifics of the job such as salary, hours, vacation time, etc. Once you find the right fit, make an offer, and if accepted, give *The Appointment Scheduler* to your new employee.

chapter 3

Consistent Scheduling

A well-trained marketing assistant can do an excellent job of scheduling appointments or making check-in calls.

To grow the business, you need a capable marketing assistant to contact and *cultivate* your client base. Clients deserve to feel appreciated, and when they are called on a regular basis, they feel valued. Keeping in touch with top prospects/clients over time can increase revenue, referrals, and your appointment stream. Your marketing assistant can help you achieve these goals.

Who makes the calls? A well-trained marketing assistant can do an excellent job of scheduling appointments or making check-in calls. I believe the only way to have a full calendar, week in and week out, is to have someone on the phone, day in and day out! If a producer can't make daily calls, then someone else on the team should make *all* the calls. Producers who insist on making their own calls are wasting valuable time.

You may be surprised at how many people agree with this approach. Despite initial reservations, producers who hire marketing assistants are rarely disappointed. In fact, they are usually delighted with their clients' positive comments. A client of mine who had been extremely reluctant to hire a marketing assistant was amazed at responses such as "Congratulations on your new employee. She did a great job on the phone," or "It's about time you hired someone to schedule your appointments."

Of course, at some point, someone is bound to complain. As an assistant, I once called a client who treated me very coldly. When I asked to schedule a review appointment with Tom, he demanded, "If Tom wants to meet with me, why doesn't he call me himself?" I replied calmly, "Tom and I work as a team. In order for Tom to spend quality time with his clients, I make all of his appointments. How does next week look for you?" My firm response placated the client, and I booked the appointment.

Developing a system. On my first day of work with Tom, I was thrown into making calls; it was definitely sink or swim! Yet I grew to love phoning. It was always a challenge to overcome an objection and to convert a "no" into an appointment. Tom's clients became *our* clients, and I enjoyed building a genuine relationship with them. Over time, my scheduling abilities helped the business grow.

Tom and I developed a successful system. No matter how busy we were, I always made the calls first thing in the morning. Clients and prospects learned our system as I called to check in, schedule an appointment, or ask for referrals. During the calls, it was clear that I honestly cared about our clients and the business.

"If you wish others to believe in you, you must first convince them that you believe in them."
Harvey Mackay

Providing the names. To be successful, marketing assistants must have a continuous flow of names to call. Without the names, the system breaks down. Where does the producer find the names for the marketing assistant?

Chapter 4

Getting the Most Out of Your Client Base

Consistent contact with clients — resulting in trust and familiarity — can lead to additional opportunities for the business.

For most producers, keeping up with their existing client base is an almost unworkable challenge. I will go out on a limb and guess that many of the names in your client base have been there since the beginning of your career. And for the most part, they have probably been ignored for several years! To improve efficiency, you should clean out your client base periodically to eliminate the dead weight.

Coding your clients. To clean out the system, start by coding your clients. How you code them is up to you, but the easiest method is A, B, or C. Your A's would be the clients who pay the most premium per year, or buy several products, or have a large net worth. The B's have the potential to become A's or to buy/invest more in the future. The C's show very little promise; you can send them an annual review letter or pass them on to another producer.

Is it unfair to pass the C's on to another producer? It would be unfair if there were absolutely *no* possibility of future business. If, however, there is even the slightest potential for business, both the producer and the C client are better off with the file transfer. The C client might appreciate some kind of contact in the future, and the producer could write some additional business.

As a consultant, I can attest to the value of reshuffling the client base. Not long ago, a client of mine had 800 people in his client base. He knew he had to lighten his load if he expected to reach the next level in his business. So he decided to get rid of his B and C clients and pare down his list to 250 key clients.

Getting the Most Out of Your Client Base

Three producers in his firm were interested in taking on his surplus clients. My client's first step was to create a percentage split for new business written in the first year. Then he sent a letter to his clients, telling them about the producers who would be servicing them from that point forward.

When clients called him with favorable reactions, he knew he had made the right decision. The process worked well for the other three producers because they ended up writing more business. Coding all the clients had been a laborious job, but in the end, the B's and C's were passed on and taken care of, and my client's revenues increased.

> *"Look at a day when you are supremely satisfied at the end. It's not a day when you lounged around doing nothing; it's when you had everything to do, and you've done it."*
>
> *Margaret Thatcher*

Review your client base. After you have created a client profile and coding system, begin the actual coding of your client base. How? First, be sure all names -- referrals, prospects, and clients -- are in the database. Second, either print the entire client list and code all the names at one time or code the names when you print your monthly call lists. (The call lists are explained later.) Doing it monthly takes six months to complete.

Either way, as you review the list, follow your profile and code each person -- A, B, or C. Judgment calls will have to be made. A few of the C's may be coded as B's because you want to keep in touch regularly. Just remember, the purpose of coding is to work your client base effectively. To avoid confusion, you may want to code the children or spouses "Q" (for quiet) so their names will not pop up on the monthly call list. Once you have coded the list, transfer the codes into the database for future call lists. I also suggest reviewing the codes yearly.

There is no magic number of A, B, or C's, but the A's are the cream of the crop, and you want to touch base with them often. (There will not be hundreds of A's.)

Preparing call lists. Once the coding is completed, you need a system to keep in touch with your clients. The key, of course, is being proactive and keeping in touch *regularly*. To produce a report, the database must have a universal connection such as the date of birth. During the third week of every month, the marketing assistant will print the names of clients who have a birthday the following month. If you want to connect twice a year, the marketing assistant should also print the names of clients who have a birthday in six months. (For example, print the September and March birthdays if you want to touch base semi-annually.) The point is to continue building relationships that could lead to new sales opportunities.

For easier access when making the calls, the marketing assistant should print the list in alphabetical order rather than by day of the month. Review the printed list with your marketing assistant to identify people to contact for an appointment or a check-in call. After the list has been reviewed, the marketing assistant will begin the calls on the first day of the following month. People will be contacted throughout the month instead of all at once. This way, your calendar will be filled with appointments throughout the month.

Check-in calls. Your marketing assistant can also make check-in calls. As I explained earlier, I believe prospects/clients should be called at least twice a year. Check-in calls take less than a minute but produce far-reaching, positive results. Clients feel better when you call periodically, without trying to sell them anything.

As an assistant, I always enjoyed making check-in calls because they gave me a chance to get to know our clients. Yes, in the beginning it was a little strained, but after a couple of calls to the same person, it became fairly easy. With regular contact, I learned firsthand about the changes in clients' lives that led directly to appointments or reviews. Clients appreciated the calls and felt they were receiving superior customer service.

With training, your marketing assistant will be able to make all the check-in calls. The best way to start a check-in call is by asking clients about a favorite topic, such as their business, family or best of all, themselves. You will be surprised at how easily people share information, especially when no appointment is at stake.

Before making a check-in call, your marketing assistant should know something about the client. If your office is well organized, the marketing assistant can get information from the files or database notes. If that is not an option, give your marketing assistant some background. Why? Because when talking with clients, marketing assistants should ask questions that pertain *specifically* to the clients. They should not ask general questions that may or may not apply to the clients' situation. In short, marketing assistants should know what they are going to say *before* they make the call.

Client changes. In time, clients will talk freely with your marketing assistant. When asked about changes, however, most clients will draw a blank They do not realize that a new address, an inheritance, additional children, or the purchase of a building or a house can create the need to review their coverage.

Once clients adapt to change, they sometimes forget about it. In other words, if a change occurred two or three months ago, and the client is accustomed to it, it's old news. Clients integrate the change into their lives so they don't remember to mention it. That is why the marketing assistant should ask about *specific* changes. Questions such as "Are you still enjoying your home in Minneapolis?" or "How are your two kids?" might prompt some discussion about changes.

After asking the questions and gathering the new information, the marketing assistant can zero in on the appointment. If a client just bought a new house, for example, the marketing assistant could say "This may be a good time for you to review with Paul. What day works for you?" If the client gives a time, schedule the appointment. If the timing isn't right, ask when a good time would be to review.

If the client suggests six months, that is perfect because his or her name will pop up at that time in your system.

If the client suggests an earlier time, sign off, and make a note to call within that time frame. Refer to Chapter Nine for a script on check-in calls.

Diversifying client interaction. In addition to check-in calls and appointment scheduling, there are several other ways to keep in touch with your client base. Let's say the monthly call list contains 50 people, and you want to see only 25 of them. What will you do with the rest? In the past, you probably ignored them, but with a routine system, you avoid cherry picking by making contact in different ways

For example, both you and your marketing assistant should be on the lookout for relevant newspaper or magazine articles for clients. The articles remind clients that you are watching out for their best interests. Also, make it a point to acknowledge special occasions and milestones. For a fiftieth birthday, a retirement, or a new business venture, send a special card. Or if you have tickets to a fun event, invite some clients. Believe me, if you show your interest, clients will be willing to meet when it's time for a review.

By making daily calls, your marketing assistant can make a big difference in your business. Consistent contact with clients -- resulting in trust and familiarity -- can lead to additional opportunities for the business.

Chapter 5

Tracking the Outcome

By tracking daily calls, marketing assistants can determine why they are not getting the right results.

Now that it's clear *why* regular calls should be made, the question is *how* to keep track of the results. A dependable system is needed to record the outcome of the daily calls.

Tracking calls. To create a system, begin with attempted calls. If a client is unavailable, your marketing assistant should make a note of it on the call list. He or she should leave a message and write the date of the message next to the client's name. (Example: 7/9) After three messages, the marketing assistant should let you know about the lack of response. You can then decide if calls should be continued or if an email or note should be sent as one last try.

Once a person is reached, the marketing assistant should jot down some notes on the call list and transfer them to the database at the end of the day. Of course, once contact is made and the notes are transferred, the person's name can be crossed off the list.

There are times when a person simply can't be reached. Whenever that happened to me, I documented my attempts in the client notes. Later, if clients called me for a service issue, I could pull their files, quickly read over the notes, and be reminded of my efforts to reach them. After helping the client, I could easily transition into asking for an appointment or discussing the reasons for my previous calls.

Client notes. Why bother with the notes? The notes provide an important reminder of what was said and when to follow up. They also help everyone stay in the loop. Client notes should be reviewed before *any* calls are made, so every team member is up to speed.

Tracking the Outcome

After all, it doesn't look good if two different people from your office call the same client on the same day about a different issue. It has happened!

As an assistant years ago, I did not have the luxury of a computer, but I did keep detailed notes in the file. After each call, I documented the date and the outcome of the call. Then before phoning again, I referred to my notes. Today, with a computer database, it is much easier to keep notes.

Tracking dials. Once you determine how many appointments you want per week, you can establish the number of calls your marketing assistant needs to make each day. The average percentages are 35% calls to reach, and 50% reached to appointments, excluding cold calls. So if the marketing assistant makes 35 calls per day, he/she should reach 12 people and make 6 appointments.

Monitoring the results of the calls is also important, especially for someone new to the scheduling process. By tracking daily calls, marketing assistants can determine why they are not getting the right results. Is the problem not enough calls, reaches, reaches to appointments, or not calling at the right time of day?

Review the numbers at least weekly in the beginning. By reviewing the numbers, you will know if the marketing assistant is doing well or if changes need to be made.

Bottom line, accountability creates habits, and habits create results. If you are not seeing an increase in quality appointments, talk to your marketing assistant about making some changes.

Tracking the Outcome

There are various ways to track daily dials, but many of them are inefficient or cumbersome. I suggest a simple one-pager that doesn't take a lot of time. In the old days I used a simple dot system so I could calculate my daily dials.

•	=	Made a call
✓	=	Reached, but no appointment made
✓̸	=	Reached and made appointment

Every time a call is made, one of the three marks (•,✓,✓̸) should be placed on the call tracking worksheet. If no message is left, use a dot. If the person is reached or the person calls back the same day, use a check mark (✓) or a check mark with two lines through it (✓̸) for an appointment. Again, if the client/prospect calls back within the same day, change the dot to a checkmark or a checkmark with two lines. If the client/prospect does not call back the same day, the dot remains. Do not go back to dots from the previous day when someone calls.

See the following page for a sample call tracking worksheet that can be copied and used on a weekly basis.

> *"A dream is just a dream. A goal is a dream with a plan and a deadline."*
>
> *Harvey Mackay*

Call Tracking Worksheet

Monday		
	_____	Calls
	_____	Reached
	_____	Appts.

Tuesday		
	_____	Calls
	_____	Reached
	_____	Appts.

Wednesday		
	_____	Calls
	_____	Reached
	_____	Appts.

Thursday		
	_____	Calls
	_____	Reached
	_____	Appts.

Friday		
	_____	Calls
	_____	Reached
	_____	Appts.

Weekly Totals:		
	_____	Calls
	_____	Reached
	_____	Appts.

Example:		
✓ ✓ ● ● ● ● ● ✗ ✗ ✗	10	Calls
	5	Reached
	3	Appts.

Tracking the Outcome

Let's recap the coding, calling, and tracking process covered in Chapters Four and Five:

1. Develop a coding system (A, B, C).
2. Put client codes in the database for future call lists.
3. Establish a uniform connection for the database (date of birth).
4. Print the call list once a month.
5. Review the call list with your marketing assistant.
6. Have your marketing assistant begin the calls in the morning on the first day of each month.
7. Make sure your marketing assistant tracks daily dials and reviews with you weekly.
8. Document the outcome of each call in the database or file.

If you follow these steps, the entire calling process should run like clockwork.

Chapter 6

Letting Go of Referral Calls

By having your marketing assistant call both referrals and existing clients, you will balance your selling opportunities.

No matter how comfortable you are delegating appointment scheduling to your marketing assistant, you might struggle with turning over your referral calls. Why? As my former employer Tom once said, "Referrals are my bread and butter. If I don't give referrals the proper attention, especially after working so hard to get them, I'll soon be out of business."

When I started with Tom, he called all the referrals himself. New to the business, he needed to gather a lot of referrals to build his client base. In the beginning, he stayed on top of the referrals with daily calling from 9:00 to 10:00 a.m. Eventually, the referrals began to pile up because we were both making appointments, and Tom's calendar was full. When it became clear that Tom no longer had time to make the referral calls, I decided to give it a try. I thought, "How difficult can it be?" I discovered very quickly that calling referrals was harder than I realized.

For one thing, it was a challenge just to reach people on the phone. And often, they already had coverage and felt their needs were met. I really had to think on my feet to keep the conversation going.

I once spoke with a referral I'll call "John" who told me that no matter what I said, he would not schedule an appointment because his job was to train telemarketers to overcome objections. "I know the drill," John said.

For a split second, I froze, but then I said with a smile, "That's great. Maybe someday you can give me a couple of tips. But today I want to find a time for you to meet with Tom. When your friend Rick gave us your name, he said you would be a tough one to crack. But he also said it would be worth a try. How does next week look for you?"

There was silence on the other end of the line, and I thought he'd hung up. "Are you still there?" I asked. John replied, "That response deserves an appointment." I promptly scheduled a time. The lesson learned that day: stay on top of the conversation and make sure people feel they are heard

When I first started working with Tom, I felt producers should make their own referral calls. I changed my mind when I saw how time-consuming the calls were. Also, Tom was often out of the office on appointments when referrals called him back. I was available and ready to take calls. All things considered, it made more sense for me to handle the referrals.

Letting go. If you are reluctant to delegate referral calls, start slowly. Say you average fifteen referrals per month. Give your marketing assistant five of them, and then gradually, add more. Over time, your marketing assistant will schedule referrals with ease.

By having your marketing assistant call both referrals and existing clients, you will balance your selling opportunities. If you are concerned that a referral will be offended, don't assume. Remember, your marketing assistant is an extension of you and is not a telemarketer or secretary. Building a relationship with prospects and clients is part of the job.

If you are fairly new to the business (three to five years), it may be easy to delegate referrals. Your focus is selling, not scheduling. If you are a veteran producer, you probably stopped asking for referrals because you lacked the time to call or because you thought you had an adequate supply of names. Either way, it is time to start asking again to build new business and to get in front of the right people. Whether you get five or twenty-five referrals in a month, they are all new opportunities.

> *"There are no secrets to success. Don't waste time looking for them. Success is the result of perfection, hard work, learning from failure, loyalty to those for whom you work, and persistence."*
> *Colin Powell*

Overcoming a referral "no." Whenever I made a referral call but didn't get the appointment, I would walk into Tom's office and recount the entire phone conversation. Sometimes, he would call the referral and say, "You just spoke with my assistant, Gina. She explained why you did not want to see me. However, (referrer) said some great things about you and felt it would be beneficial for us to meet." In most cases, Tom did not get the appointment either which made me feel less deflated. But if he did, I learned new techniques from the call.

As I mentioned earlier, it is pretty easy to keep a producer in front of existing clients. But the marketing assistants who get results when contacting a broad range of people -- referrals, prospects, existing clients or even cold calls -- become income generators. Why? Because when the calendar is filled consistently with sales opportunities, revenue is bound to increase.

Once you truly let go of making calls, your calendar will be filled with as many appointments as *you* want. So let go, be patient, and spend more time meeting with clients and selling. Let your marketing assistant schedule *all* the appointments.

Chapter 7

Telephoning Fundamentals

The key to successful appointment scheduling is learning to control the outcome of the call.

One way to reduce the unpredictability of appointment scheduling is to use our scripts, at least in the beginning. Whether your marketing assistant is an absolute beginner or a seasoned pro, telephoning techniques are always helpful. The key to successful appointment scheduling is learning to control the outcome of the call. In other words, marketing assistants can manage the call by getting to the point, remaining persistent, and assuming they will get the appointments.

The approach. The marketing assistant should be friendly, but not phony, and firm but not pushy, remembering that the marketing assistant *sells the appointment*, while the producer sells the product or service. Yes, marketing assistants should know the general nature of the appointment and the producer's specialty, but their job is to fill the calendar.

Keep it simple. Some producers want marketing assistants to use flashy words or go into detail about tax savings benefits, etc. I believe the best approach is to keep it simple and just ask for the appointment. Why? If someone asks questions about specific products or services, the marketing assistant might not have the answers. The phone call could become awkward.

I also recommend brevity. If the marketing assistant rambles on, the message is lost. Get to the point, and people will respond.

With our scripts, marketing assistants avoid long-winded spiels that sound unnatural. Of course, other approaches are acceptable, but this language works because it is simple and to the point. Once they are experienced, marketing assistants can jump through any hoops without the scripts.

Telephoning Fundamentals

A friendly voice makes a difference. When making phone calls, there is one variable that marketing assistants can control at all times: their voice. People respond to a friendly voice, which means tone and inflection really do make a difference. When a caller is upbeat, people tend to listen.

Introductions. For any type of call, the introduction is key. It is what captures the attention of the person on the other end of the line. If marketing assistants are enthusiastic and concise, they will get better results; excess verbiage can lead to a phone hang up. Marketing assistants also need to inject some life into the conversation and not sound robotic. Their goal is to generate interest without sounding like they're reading.

Verbal ping pong. Asking for an appointment is similar to playing a game of ping pong -- polite, verbal ping pong. The marketing assistant begins with an introduction, and then asks for the appointment. After the request for an appointment, the ball is in the other person's court. When the person hits the ball back with an objection, the rally begins. When the marketing assistant asks for the appointment again, the ball goes back to the other court. The objective is to keep asking for the appointment.

Listening skills required. A successful phone call also requires listening skills. Marketing assistants need to *hear* the person on the other end of the line. When an objection is made, they should counter it appropriately. If a person says "I am not interested," the response would be "We didn't assume you would be at this time."

If the person says "I am busy," the reply would be "I can appreciate that," or "I understand," or "When would be a better time for you?"

> *"Many people may listen, but few people actually hear."*
>
> Harvey Mackay

Persistence pays off. It is important to be personable and *persistent*. Being persistent means asking for the appointment repeatedly in a pleasant way. Every time the person objects, the marketing assistant should overcome the objection, then ask for the appointment again by repeating "How does your schedule look?" or "How does next week look?" or "When would be a good time for you?"

There is also a huge difference between asking for an appointment and asking *permission* for an appointment. Asking for the appointment: "How does next week look for you?" Asking permission: "Is it okay to schedule an appointment for next week?"

I remember a situation with a referral I will call "Bill." I called Bill repeatedly, left numerous messages, but never managed to connect with him. One day I finally reached him. I was very enthusiastic because I actually had him on the line. Bill did not feel the same way!

After my introduction, he shut me down quickly, saying he wasn't interested. When I asked, "What aren't you interested in?" he replied, "Whatever you're selling."

I told Bill I wasn't selling anything, but was trying to set up a time for Tom to meet him. Again, he said he wasn't interested. I didn't give up because despite his emphatic *no*, Bill was talkative. After four objections (polite, verbal ping pong), I felt I might have pushed Bill too far. I heard him pound his fist on his desk and say, "When does he want to see me?" I paused for a nanosecond -- I didn't want to lose him -- and replied, "How's next Wednesday for you?"

The appointment was scheduled but I thought Bill would cancel. To my surprise, he didn't. When Tom walked into Bill's office, Bill said, "I don't know how much you're paying your assistant, but it better be good. The only reason you're here is because she wouldn't let me off the phone without making an appointment." Tom just smiled and began the meeting.

Every time I called Bill, he was a tough customer, but he appreciated my approach because it convinced him to do what was right for his family and him. I am not saying you should be overly aggressive on the phone, but a little persistence goes a long way.

> *"Be like a postage stamp. Stick to it until you get there."*
>
> *Harvey Mackay*

Telephoning Fundamentals

Remember, marketing assistants need to be in control of the phone call. My advice: take charge, be confident, and stick to it to get results. Because marketing assistants rarely know what to expect from the person on the other end of the line, our scripts help them overcome resistance and develop the confidence to ask repeatedly for the appointment. It does not matter what type of call is made -- marketing assistants need to be ready for whatever comes their way.

Chapter 8

Practice Makes Perfect

With practice, marketing assistants become more confident and develop a real flair over the phone.

The beauty of *The Appointment Scheduler* is that it simplifies the scheduling process. By using the scripts and making calls every day, marketing assistants develop a routine that leads to success. Again, the goal is clear: getting the producer in front of the right people at the right time on a regular basis.

Practice with phone scripts. Chapter Nine contains phone scripts for calling and handling objections to the appointment. The *sample* dialogue will help marketing assistants discover what works best for them.

Another service provided by #O.N.E. CONCEPTS is a training program for marketing assistants. During our telephone training sessions, I ask the marketing assistants to tape record the role-playing. By taping the sessions, the marketing assistants are less distracted during the call. They aren't trying to take notes and catch every word I say.

It is important for marketing assistants to practice the language before tackling the phone. I recommend purchasing a hand-held micro-cassette recorder to help with role-playing. Marketing assistants can rehearse the language in order to sound more natural. By practicing and recording on a micro-cassette (just forget the machine is on), they become more comfortable with the scripts. They can hear their "ums" and "ahs" and notice when they are rambling. Rewinding the tape helps them determine how and where to improve. With practice, marketing assistants become more confident and develop a real flair over the phone.

The value of role-playing. I recently worked with a new marketing assistant I will call "Nicole."

Practice Makes Perfect

The first role-playing session was a difficult phone call for both of us. Nicole was very wordy and stiff which meant I had to give her constructive criticism. I asked her to eliminate excess verbiage, sound more energetic, and most important, keep asking for the appointment. She became increasingly frustrated with me.

By the end of the call, Nicole was drained. Two weeks later, we had our second role-playing session. I was amazed at Nicole's progress and told her so. She replied, "While I was on the phone with you, I thought I was doing just fine. I could not understand why you were trying to change my approach. But later, when I listened to the tape, I realized how long-winded I was. After that, I wanted to improve."

For many marketing assistants, the role-playing tapes are a revelation. They hear how they actually sound during their practice phone calls and realize they can do better. It is not unusual for marketing assistants to pull out the tapes months later for a quick refresher and confidence booster.

Role-playing is a useful teaching tool. Encourage your marketing assistant to start practicing with the scripts in Chapter Nine!

"Energy and persistence conquer all things."
Benjamin Franklin

Chapter 9

Scripts for Success

The goal is for you to own this language, so it feels completely comfortable.

*(Author's Note: In Chapters Nine, Ten, and Eleven, **I** **offer advice directly to the marketing assistants**. The marketing assistants should read the chapters carefully and then follow the recommendations. Producers should read these three chapters, as well.)*

The scripts in this chapter will help you close the deal, which in this case means schedule an appointment. The goal is for you to own this language, so it feels completely comfortable. The more you practice, the better you will sound. Eventually, you will feel relaxed and confident, and as a result, you will get the appointment. Once you are comfortable with the various approaches, you can use them interchangeably for any type of phone call.

To make the scripts easier to follow, we have included names for each person and business. Start practicing!

REFERRAL LANGUAGE

Marketing Assistant = Megan
Producer = Paul Armstrong
Referrer = Rick Doe
Business = XYZ Financial

Introductions

Hello. This is Megan with Paul Armstrong's office at XYZ Financial. How are you today? Rick Doe mentioned your name to us and thought you would benefit from meeting with Paul. How does your schedule look?

or

Hello. This is Megan with Paul Armstrong's office at XYZ Financial. Our client, Rick Doe, suggested we give you a call for an opportunity to meet with Paul. How does next Thursday look?

or

Hi, this is Megan with Paul Armstrong's office at XYZ Financial. Rick Doe, a client of ours, thought you would benefit from meeting with Paul. How does next week look for you?

OVERCOMING REFERRAL OBJECTIONS

"Not interested"

We didn't assume you were in the market at this time. The first meeting with Paul is to introduce himself and the services we offer. How does next week look?

"I am too busy"

I can appreciate that. When would be a good time for you to meet with Paul?

"This is not a good time"

When would be a better time for you? Rick said some great things about you, and Paul is looking forward to meeting with you.

"I already have a financial person"

That's great, but when Rick gave us your name, he felt you could get some new ideas from Paul. He will be in your area on Wednesday. How does that work for you?

"I don't need insurance/investments"

We didn't assume you were in the market to make any changes at this time. Paul would just like the opportunity to introduce himself and explain the services he offers. How does your schedule look?

"I have a friend (or relative) in the business"

That's great. We didn't assume you were looking to make a change at this time. Sometime in the future, when you want to make some changes, it might be helpful to know more about our approach. How does next week look for you?

"Just mail me the information"

Everyone's situation is different. To really make the information useful to you, Paul would like to meet in person and explain the services we offer. How does next week look for you?

"I can't afford anything at this time"

We didn't assume you were in the market to purchase anything at this time. During the meeting, Paul will explain the services we offer so if and when you decide to make any changes, you will know more about us. Does morning or afternoon work better for you?

"I have enough coverage already"

I understand, and quite frankly, we'd be surprised if someone like you didn't. We handle a variety of products and services that may be helpful in the future. When Rick mentioned your name, he thought you would enjoy meeting with Paul. He will be in your area next week. How does Tuesday look?

EXISTING CLIENT REVIEW LANGUAGE

Marketing Assistant = Megan
Producer = Paul Armstrong
Business = XYZ Financial

Introductions

Hello. This is Megan with Paul Armstrong's office at XYZ Financial. How are you today? Paul would like the opportunity to review with you. How does your schedule look?

or

Hi, this is Megan with Paul Armstrong's office at XYZ Financial. It's time for your annual review. When would be a good time in your schedule?

or

Hi, this is Megan with Paul Armstrong's office at XYZ Financial. It's been a while since your last review, and Paul would like to spend about a half hour with you. How does next week look?

OVERCOMING REVIEW OBJECTIONS

"Nothing has changed"

We didn't assume there were any changes. However, it's been a while since your last review, and Paul wanted to be sure everything is up to date. How does your schedule look?

"I am too busy"

I can appreciate that. When would be a good time for you to review with Paul?

"Call back in two weeks"

I would be more than happy to do that. (*Or, I have his schedule here.*) How does the week of the 23rd work for you?

"This is not a good time"

When would be a better time for you? It's been a year since your last review, and Paul wants to spend about a half hour with you.

"There's no need to review"

We didn't assume there were any changes, but Paul likes to meet with his clients at least once a year. Does next week work for you?

"I am working with someone else now"

I am sorry to hear that. You still have coverage with us, and it would be to your benefit to make sure it's up to date. When would be a good time for you?

"Why does he want to review?"
It's been a while since your last review, and he wants to be sure everything is up to date. What day works best for you?

CHECK-IN CALL INTRODUCTIONS

Hello, this is Megan with Paul Armstrong's office at XYZ Financial. I am calling to see if there have been any changes or anything we should be doing for you at this time. Are you still living at (address)?

or

Hi, this is Megan with Paul Armstrong's office at XYZ Financial. I am calling to wish you a happy birthday. Are you having a good day? While I have you on the telephone, I would like to update your file.

or

Hello, this is Megan with Paul Armstrong's office at XYZ Financial. As you know, we call you twice a year to keep our records up to date. Are there any changes or anything we should be doing for you at this time?

or

Hello, this is Megan with Paul Armstrong's office at XYZ Financial. How are you? Has anything changed since your last meeting with Paul?

Know the situation. Be sure you know something about your client's personal situation to avoid asking questions that don't apply. In other words, don't ask someone in her sixties if she recently had a child. Here are some sample questions for a check-in call:

Scripts for Success

Address

"Are you still at the same address?"
Follow-up question =
"Did you buy a new home or are you renting?"

Marriage

"Any change in your marital status?"
Follow-up question =
"What is your spouse's name and date of birth?"

Children

"Do you have any (more) children?"
Follow-up question =
"Congratulations. What is the baby's name? When was the baby born?"

Outside Coverage

"When did you get outside coverage?"
Follow-up question =
"What company are you working with? May I ask what you purchased?"

Inheritance

"Any changes in your family situation?"
Follow-up question =
"Have you moved the money yet? Where?"

SEMINAR FOLLOW-UP LANGUAGE

Marketing Assistant = Megan
Producer = Paul Armstrong
Business = XYZ Financial

Introductions

Hello, this is Megan with Paul Armstrong's office at XYZ Financial. How are you today? Thank you for attending our seminar. We hope you enjoyed it. I would like to schedule a time for you to meet with Paul. How does next week look for you?

or

Hi, this is Megan with Paul Armstrong's office at XYZ Financial. You recently attended our seminar, and Paul would like the opportunity to meet with you sometime next week. How does your schedule look?

or

Hello, this is Megan with Paul Armstrong's office at XYZ Financial. I am calling to schedule a follow-up meeting after the seminar. When would be a good time for you to meet with Paul?

OVERCOMING SEMINAR FOLLOW-UP OBJECTIONS

"I received enough information at the seminar"
That's great. This meeting helps you clarify your personal and financial goals and is all about you, which means it's not a sales pitch. At the end of the meeting, you will be clear on what's important to you during retirement or in the future. How does next week look for you?

"I am not interested"
This one-on-one meeting gives you the opportunity to learn more about the services we provide, and there's no commitment on your part. How does your schedule look?

"I am already working with someone"
Most of our existing clients were working with someone before meeting with us. If you get some additional ideas, it may be worth your time. How does next week look for you?

"I can't afford to make any changes"
We didn't assume you were going to do anything at this time. Paul wants to follow up with all seminar attendees to explain our services.

"Now is not a good time for me"
I can appreciate that. When would be a good time for you to meet with Paul?

COLD CALL LANGUAGE

Marketing Assistant = Megan
Producer = Paul Armstrong
Business = XYZ Financial

Introductions

Hello, this is Megan with Paul Armstrong's office at XYZ Financial. How are you today? I am calling to schedule a time for you to meet with Paul to learn about a unique retirement plan (*or insert the producer's specialty*). How does your schedule look?

or

Hello, this is Megan with Paul Armstrong's office at XYZ Financial. I know you're busy, so I won't take much of your time. Paul works with (*business owners/doctors/professionals*) like yourself, specializing in business succession planning. I am calling to schedule a time for you two to meet. When would be a good time for you?

or

Hello, this is Megan with Paul Armstrong's office at XYZ Financial. Paul has worked with (*business owners/doctors/professionals*) like yourself for several years and would like the opportunity to stop by, introduce himself, and tell you about his services. How does next week look for you?

or

Hi, this is Megan with Paul Armstrong's office at XYZ Financial. Paul has worked with (*business owners/ doctors/professionals*) like yourself for several years and would like the opportunity to meet with you. How does next week look?

OVERCOMING COLD CALL OBJECTIONS

"I am not interested"

We didn't assume you would be. But Paul would still like to meet with you to share some valuable opportunities for you to think about. If or when you need these services, you will know something about Paul. How does next week look for you?

"What are you selling?"

At XYZ Financial, we never push a particular product. We identify your needs and review what you are currently doing. Then we make suggestions that fit your needs.

"It's not a good time"

I can appreciate that. When would be a better time for you?

"I already have an insurance/retirement plan"

We didn't assume you wanted to make any changes, but we would still like the opportunity to meet with you to tell you about our services. How does your schedule look?

"I don't need anything right now"

The first time Paul meets with you is to explain the services he offers. If your needs change in the future, you'll know about us. How does your schedule look?

Scripts for Success

"I am satisfied with what I have"
or "I don't have any money"

We didn't assume that you needed to make any changes now. We'd just like the opportunity to meet you, explain the services we provide, and share some tax saving ideas with you. When would be a good time for you to meet with Paul?

"I already have a financial planner"

That's great! However, we'd still like the opportunity to meet with you to review the services we provide. When would be a good time to meet with Paul?

"I am really busy"

I can appreciate that. When would be a better time for you to meet with Paul?

"What kind of plans are you talking about?"

Our firm offers many services and that's why Paul would like to meet with you to better understand your situation. How does your schedule look next week?

"No"

May I ask why not?

Chapter 10

Every Call Counts

Your professionalism -- the way you leave messages, return calls, confirm appointments, and get past gate-keepers -- has a significant impact on the business.

During phone calls, there are specific situations in which a trained marketing assistant can make a real difference. Your professionalism -- the way you leave messages, return calls, confirm appointments, and get past gatekeepers -- has a significant impact on the business. The scenarios below will help you create a favorable impression on current and potential clients.

Leaving messages. Leaving messages is an important step toward increasing your appointment ratios. If you make the calls first thing in the morning, people have all day to reach you. Ideally, messages should be left every three to four days to create a sense of urgency.

When leaving a message, *be brief.* You increase the odds of a return call if you keep things general and skip the details. If you indicate why you are calling -- i.e., to schedule an appointment -- people might not call back because they do not feel they need to review. An appropriate message would be "Hi John, this is Megan with Paul Armstrong's office at XYZ Financial. Please call me at 952-555-1234. I look forward to hearing from you."

Each time you leave a message with the same person, mix it up a little to avoid sounding monotonous or programmed. The second message would be "Hi John, this is Megan again with Paul Armstrong's office at XYZ Financial. I haven't heard back from you so I thought I would try again. Please call me at 952-555-1234. Have a great day!"

The third message: "Hi John, this is Megan with Paul Armstrong's office at XYZ Financial. I need to touch base with you on a couple of things and would appreciate a return call. Please call me at 952-555-1234 at your earliest convenience. I look forward to talking with you."

If you do not get a return call after three tries, talk to your producer or put in a reminder to try again in six months. Whatever you decide, be sure to document in your notes that the person did not return your call.

Occasionally, you will have a client's home phone number instead of a daytime number. In those situations, leave this message: "Hi, this is Megan from XYZ Financial. I am sorry to call you at home, but I don't have your daytime phone number. Please feel free to call me this evening at 952-555-1234 to let me know how to reach you during the day. I look forward to hearing from you." Or, "Sorry I missed you. I don't have a phone number to call you during the day. If you would call me this evening with a daytime number, I would appreciate it. I am at 952-555-1234. I look forward to speaking to you."

Returned calls. If a person *does* call back, make the most of it. Usually, when people return calls, they apologize for not getting back sooner. This is your opportunity to say, "I understand you are very busy, and I appreciate your return call. In the future, just call me and say that it's not a good time for you. Then we can figure out a better time to connect. I don't want to waste your time going back and forth with messages."

During the call, you can also lay the groundwork for future communication. If cherry picking was the norm in the past, and now a new system is in place, inform clients how and when they will be called in the future. If you try to schedule an appointment and the person continues to put you off, here are some effective responses to the evasions:

"I'll call you back"
Great. If I don't hear from you, when should I try you again?

"No desire to get together"
Things have a way of changing. When would be a better time to call again?

"Call me back at a later date"
I would be more than happy to do so. When is the best time for me to try back?

Dead weight. If you call a prospect or client over and over and do not get results, it may be time to clean out the system. What does this mean? It means getting rid of the dead weight -- i.e., the people who are never going to make changes, including A and B clients -- and putting the focus on key clients, where it belongs.

The quiet file. If clients will not review, ask some questions to see if they would prefer to be in the inactive system or "quiet file." The quiet file is for people who do not want to be contacted on a regular basis; they will call you when they need you. To set up the inactive system, simply ask if people want to be called in the future. If they don't, they go into the quiet file. If they do, they need to make an appointment.

Remember, there's only so much time in a day. You should concentrate on people who believe in what you do and who are serious about their future.

Here are some responses to clients who are candidates for the quiet file:

"I don't want to meet"
Would you prefer to be in our inactive system, which means we will wait to hear from you?

"Yes, put me in the inactive system"
Thank you for your time and please call us if you need anything in the future.

"No, I don't want to be in the inactive system"
I understand, and in order to keep in touch with you, I need to schedule a review appointment. When would be a good time for you?

Solidifying the appointment. When you do make an appointment, it is important to end the call by repeating the arrangements. You can confirm the day, time, and location of the appointment by saying, "Great, I have you down for (day), (time), and (location). Please call me at 952-555-1234 if something changes. We look forward to seeing you then."

Or if the producer is going to the client's office or home, confirm by saying, "Paul looks forward to seeing you then."

Confirming appointments. If you provide a written confirmation or a reminder call for the appointment, do not mention it after scheduling an appointment. You want to be sure people put the appointment on their calendar. Sometimes if a reminder is offered, people rely on it, and then when they are called to confirm, they cancel the appointment.

If you do confirm an appointment by telephone, do not sound tentative. Present the appointment as a firm commitment. Instead of saying, "I am calling to remind you of your appointment tomorrow at 2:00 p.m. Does that still work for you?" try this: "We look forward to seeing you tomorrow at 2:00 p.m. Have a great day."

The first version sounds conditional, while the second one presents the appointment as a definite go.

Getting past the gatekeepers. To schedule appointments with referrals, prospects, or cold calls, you may have to get past a gatekeeper. The gatekeeper has been trained to keep sales types away from the boss. Getting past this human barrier can be more difficult than actually making an appointment with the person you are calling.

An assistant, receptionist, or office manager/gatekeeper can actually become your ally. Getting to know them helps you get in the door. Ask for their names so you may address them personally in the future. Using first names makes people feel appreciated and will increase your chances of getting help or information. Remember, treat the gatekeeper the way *you* want to be treated when you are dealing with an incoming call.

I encountered my share of gatekeepers when I worked with Tom. Because Tom did a lot of business with lawyers, I called a certain Chicago law office several times a week. We had clients there who called back regularly whenever I left messages. One day I realized some of my calls were not being returned. This had never happened before. Concerned about the unreturned calls, I dropped a note to an existing client to make sure everything was OK. After receiving my note, he called to say he never got my phone messages. Apparently, a new receptionist thought I was a telemarketer and did not take my calls seriously.

I phoned the receptionist, introduced myself, and explained the reason for my calls. She apologized and promised it would never happen again -- and it didn't. The next time Tom went to that office, I arranged for him to give the receptionist a bouquet of flowers. He introduced himself, and from that point on, she was a tremendous help to both of us.

Clearly, there are ways to get around a diligent gatekeeper if you are creative. Here are some ideas:

1. Call first thing in the morning, during the lunch hour, or late in the day when gatekeepers are not at their desks. In some cases, the person you are calling will answer the phone.

2. When calling a referral, mention the name of the referrer who suggested the call. The gatekeeper will probably recognize the name of the referrer and take the message, or will direct your call.

3. Create a sense of urgency with your voice: "Hi, this is Megan with Paul Armstrong's office at XYZ Financial. Rick Doe said we should contact Ron Carter right away. Is he in?"

4. If you leave several messages without a return call, try this: "Ron Carter is impossible to reach, and there is no point in leaving another message. When is the best time to call back?" When you get an answer, tell the gatekeeper you will call back on that day and time, and ask to have the call penciled in on the calendar. Also, remind the gatekeeper to mention that Rick Doe (the referrer) suggested you call.

5. After leaving a couple of messages, voicemail can be a way in. If you do not receive a return call despite several messages, leave a detailed message: "Hi Ron, this is Megan from Paul Armstrong's office at XYZ Financial. I am sure you are very busy since I did not hear back from you. Rick Doe said some great things about you and felt you would benefit from meeting with Paul. Please return my call to schedule a time for you and Paul to meet. I look forward to hearing from you."

Again, treat the gatekeeper with courtesy and respect, and you increase the odds of reaching the referral or prospect.

Chapter 11

Additional Opportunities

Expanding the role of the marketing assistant makes financial sense.

Once you are comfortable on the phone, there are endless opportunities for new business development. Asking for referrals, strategizing with a center of influence, identifying new opportunities during a check-in call -- all can lead to more business. Expanding the role of the marketing assistant makes financial sense.

Increasing referral opportunities. Eventually, you can ask for referrals during a check-in call or when a client calls in for service. Generally speaking, it is the producer's job to ask for the referrals, but if you also ask, there will be more names to call and more potential for business. Ideally, you will ask for referrals once you get to know the client base and feel comfortable doing so.

Examples of asking for referrals during check-in or service calls:

Thank you for the introduction to John Jones. We had the opportunity to meet with him, and the meeting went well. Can you think of anyone else who would benefit from our services?

or

You have always been good about giving us referrals, and we appreciate that. Is there anyone else you know who could benefit from a meeting with us?

or

You referred us to John Jones. We had an opportunity to meet, and he did some business with us. Who else do you know who would benefit from our services?

or

Do you know anyone who recently had a child, was promoted, is newly married, just retired, or is a new associate in the company?

or

As you know, we work by referrals only. Has the firm hired any new associates lately?

or

As you know, we work by referrals only. Who do you know that would benefit from our services?

Referral process. The producer should also ask for referrals during every meeting. To remind the producer, you can create a referral sheet to collect basic information such as name, address, and *work* telephone number. A referral sheet is more efficient than a random Post-It note and can be kept in the client file for future reference.

When I worked with Tom, I placed a referral sheet in every file before every appointment. Because Tom was so good at asking for referrals, the sheet usually came back completely filled out. If the referrer could not think of anyone at the time, Tom would leave the referral sheet and I would follow up with a phone call a week later.

In either case, once I transferred the information, I kept the referral sheet in the client file. I always wrote down the month and year we received the referrals and then tracked the outcome of our calls once I connected with the referral. Prior to my monthly calls, I reviewed the sheets and updated clients on the outcome of their referrals. This way, clients were comfortable about giving us more referrals.

Additional Opportunities

As we all know, asking for referrals is not easy. Many producers do not ask for them because they fear rejection, run out of time during a meeting, or don't have time to make the calls. The referral sheets and follow-up calls make the process much easier.

Our referral sheet was relatively simple. At the top, it indicated the type of clients we worked with (e.g., attorneys, accountants, physicians). There was space for three separate referrals. The information we requested included name, company, address, business phone number, and email address. An example of a referral sheet can be found on page 106.

Tracking a Center of Influence (COI). Another great source of referrals is a Center of Influence (COI), a well-connected person who is in touch with the producer on a regular basis. The best way to maintain a solid relationship with a COI is to have a systematic tracking process. Whether there are five or twenty-five COIs, the relationships are important for referrals.

To track COIs, I recommend creating an Excel spreadsheet with a total of 16 columns. The columns are: COIs, the COIs' phone numbers, the 12 months of the year (each month, January through December, has its own column), referral names, and results. List your current COIs in alphabetical order; then, whenever you get a new one, add the name.

An Excel spreadsheet provides a system to track your actions with the COIs and any referrals they give. At the end of each month, when you are reviewing the call list with the producer, discuss the type of action to take with the COIs. Each month you will update the spreadsheet

REFERRAL SHEET

I'd appreciate your help! Please suggest people you know -- friends, doctors, associates, attorneys, accountants, or sales professionals -- who could benefit from meeting with me to learn more about my services.

1. Name:_____

    Company:_____

    Address:_____

    Business #:_____

    Email:_____

2. Name:_____

    Company:_____

    Address:_____

    Business #:_____

    Email:_____

3. Name:_____

    Company:_____

    Address:_____

    Business #:_____

    Email:_____

Please fax to:

Additional Opportunities

with information on what the producer did, if anything (golf, lunch at the country club, or a handwritten note).

Each time someone is referred by the COI, write the name in the referral name box. Track the outcome of the referrals in the result column. Then, at the end of the year, you will know if creative connections paid off with referrals.

If they did not, remove the names from the spreadsheet and make sure the producer cultivates a stronger relationship with the people who are providing referrals. Take advantage of these additional opportunities to grow the business. By handling the referral calls and COIs, you will become an indispensable part of the sales cycle.

A example of a COI spreadsheet can be found on the following page.

Center of Influence	Phone #	Jan. through Dec. (one column per month)											Referrals	Results

Chapter 12

Telephone Prep and Procedures

Confident marketing assistants can move the business forward.

Daily phone calls by the marketing assistant are a crucial part of the sales cycle. As an assistant, I learned the importance of being prepared and following a daily routine. Without a system, it is easy to veer off course.

Here are some suggestions and reminders to keep you focused on the telephoning process.

- Review the telephone scripts frequently. Practice them out loud.
- Role-play as often as possible. Practice makes perfect.
- Record your role-playing sessions. Listen to the tapes to improve your methods and monitor progress.
- Be ready to make calls in the morning during an uninterrupted stretch of time.
- Call referrals, prospects, and clients at daytime phone numbers whenever possible.
- At the end of every month, meet with the producer to review the upcoming call lists.
- Establish daily call goals. Goal = make 35 dials, reach 12 people, make 6 appointments.
- Remember, the goal on the telephone is to get the appointment. Ask for the appointment, not the sale.
- Keep files or call lists on your desk in alphabetical order for easy access when someone returns your call.
- Leave a message if the referral, prospect, or client is unavailable.

Telephone Prep and Procedures

- After leaving three messages with no response, discuss the outcome with your producer.
- When calling to make an appointment, assume you will get the appointment. If you convey confidence, you will get results.
- When an appointment is made, end the conversation by reconfirming the day, time, and place of the appointment.
- Keep track of dials on a daily basis. At the end of every month, review your numbers with your producer.
- Before each check-in call, read the client notes, if available, to learn more about the client's situation.
- During check-in calls, ask specific questions to uncover new opportunities.
- Use your most powerful sales tool -- your voice.
- Be confident. You are providing a valuable service to your clients and prospects.
- Ask for referrals during check-in calls or when someone calls in for service.

Confident marketing assistants can move the business forward. Follow these suggestions and you will enjoy additional opportunities for growth.

Conclusion

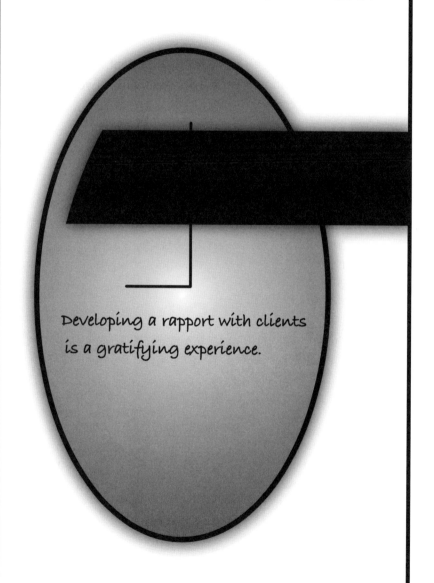

Developing a rapport with clients
is a gratifying experience.

When I was an assistant, I loved being on the phone, and it showed in my results. In addition to building the business, I made new friends and conducted interesting conversations that made a huge impact on my life.

As you begin making phone calls, remember that your role is important to the financial future of the business. It is also crucial to the financial well-being of the clients. If we don't remind clients to come in for a review or explain to prospects how a producer can help, these people may not be protected against life's tragedies.

After years of telephoning Tom's clients, I discovered an important truth: my calls really made a difference. People appreciated the personal touch and as a result, they were more inclined to do business with us. Some clients -- for instance, the ones who later became uninsurable -- were especially grateful for our consistent calls because we'd made sure they had sufficient coverage. Developing a rapport with clients is a gratifying experience.

Bottom line, our clients appreciated my calls and let me know it. The interesting part is how they knew my efforts went beyond business. Clients could tell that I honestly cared about them. To my astonishment, after I left Tom's employ, several of them called me on *my* birthday to check in with me. It was their way of saying thank you.

I wish you great success as you perfect your systems and telephoning skills. I hope you reach the point where you enjoy the calls as much as I did. Keep dialing!

CALL TO ACTION

What can you do *today* to improve your business? Call us at 952-829-5300 to sign up for an individual training program or a group seminar. We offer a series of one-on-one training calls as well as a comprehensive telephoning seminar for marketing assistants. In both sessions, marketing assistants learn to:

- Understand the game plan to work the client base
- Keep client notes
- Overcome obstacles in setting appointments
- Make check-in calls
- Monitor results from daily calls
- Convert service calls into sales opportunities
- Ask for referrals
- Coordinate and track centers of influence

One-On-One Training -- The Calendar Enhancer

The art of the phone call – that's what *The Calendar Enhancer* teaches marketing assistants who want to sharpen their telephone techniques. Our one-on-one role-playing sessions over the phone help marketing assistants gain the confidence to schedule more appointments, ask for referrals, and develop a real rapport with clients. The sessions are specially tailored to meet the needs of the marketing assistant and the producer.

Group Training -- **The Calendar Enhancer Seminar**

The Calendar Enhancer Seminar is the perfect opportunity for marketing assistants to improve their skills in an intensive, one-day session. All aspects of telephoning are covered in the seven-hour class. Scripts and role-playing are used to teach techniques that can help marketing assistants schedule appointments with quality prospects and clients.

If private instruction is preferred, the one-on-one sessions are recommended. In the group training, marketing assistants learn from each other as well as from us.

At #O.N.E. CONCEPTS, we provide consulting services, products, and publications for the financial services industry. Our specialty is helping business owners:

- Improve productivity and morale
- Clarify work responsibilities
- Build strong teams
- Avoid duplicated efforts
- Optimize team capabilities
- Strengthen leadership skills
- Revamp work habits
- Maximize productivity and profits
- Set clear-cut goals
- Tackle the hiring process
- Streamline office procedures

We work with clients throughout the United States and Canada. If you need help with small business management and employee development, give us a call today!

#O.N.E. CONCEPTS
It takes the team to go the distance.

How to Reach Us

SERVICES
The Movitational Method
The Calendar Enhancer
The Personnel Package

TELECONFERENCES
The Hiring Method
The TeamWork Approach

SEMINARS
The TeamWork Cycle
The Calendar Enhancer
The Power of TeamWork
The Speaker Forum

PUBLICATIONS
The Personnel Package
The Power of Two (out of print)
The Appointment Scheduler

Pellegrini Team Consulting
8945 Aztec Drive
Eden Prairie, MN 55347
(952) 829-5300
www.pellegriniteam.com

Gina Pellegrini has worked in the financial services industry for nearly thirty years. After a successful career as an assistant with a top insurance producer in Chicago, she started her own national consulting firm, #O.N.E. CONCEPTS. Based in Minneapolis, Gina and her team help clients streamline their businesses, improve teamwork, build leadership skills, hire qualified employees, and schedule more appointments.

Gina is also a coach for The Strategic Coach program based in Toronto, Canada.

INDEX